pablo the peacock

A story about attention seeking

By Steve Blakesley
Illustrated by Natalie Griffiths

LDA

Pablo was a peacock,
With a blue-gold spangled tail.
His many coloured feathers,
Could fan out like a sail.

He loved to hear the children gasp,
To see his great display.
And the admiring public,
Who came on Open Day.

If children would not look at him,
He made a raucous cry.
He thought it sounded wonderful,
For the people passing by.

He knew he was impressive,
The star of every show.
He was the most important bird,
And told everybody so.

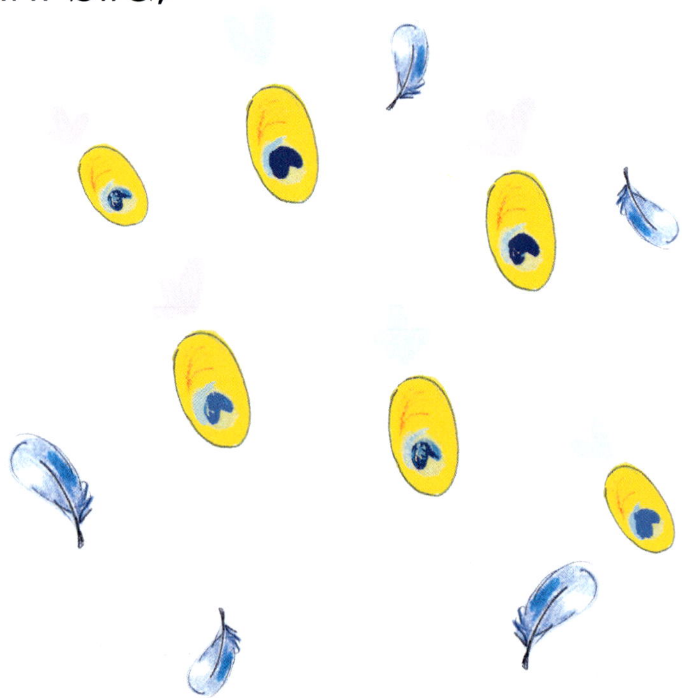

One morning Pablo noticed,
There was a great 'to do'.
A massive stage and bunting,
And a splendid brass band too.

He stretched out all his feathers,
And screeched his famous song.
But though the staff all turned to look,
They didn't stare that long.

Some visitors were coming,
To Chester Abbey Park.
For the opening of a petting zoo,
A hands-on Noah's Ark.

With red carpet spread across the stage,
And microphones as well.
For Meghan and Prince Harry,
So they didn't have to yell.

But Pablo didn't like this,
And almost on a whim.
He flew right up upon the stage,
So all could look at him.

A keeper went to shoo him,
But the bird could not care less.
And Pablo got quite cross with him,
And promptly dumped a mess.

The keepers caught him neatly,
And Pablo felt the rage.
But they were having none of it,
And put him in a cage.

He screamed his cry aloud again,
Showed off his tail extension.
But no one had the time for him,
They paid him no attention.

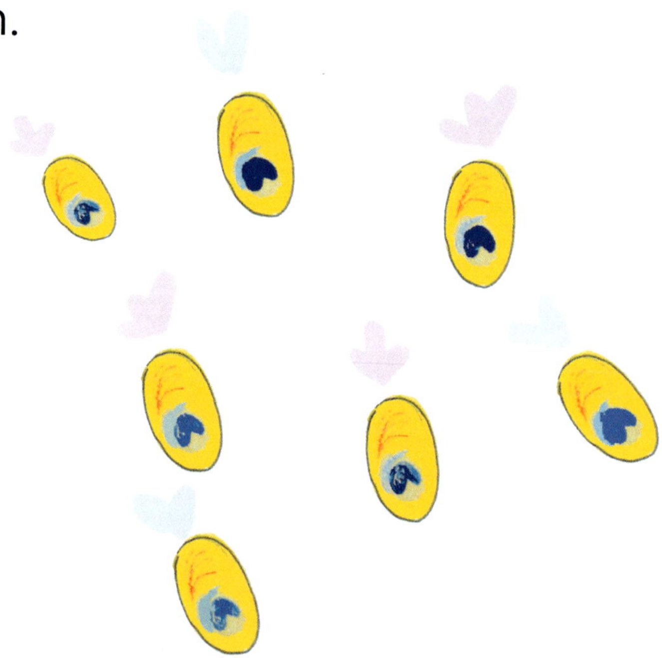

Prince Harry came with Meghan,
And made a cracking speech.
While Pablo in his private cage,
Let out a massive screech.

And then the royal party,
Were shown around the zoo.
To see the calves and guinea pigs,
And all the ducklings too.

At last they came to Pablo's cage,
And Pablo gave a wail.
He strutted over to the prince,
And spread his glorious tail.

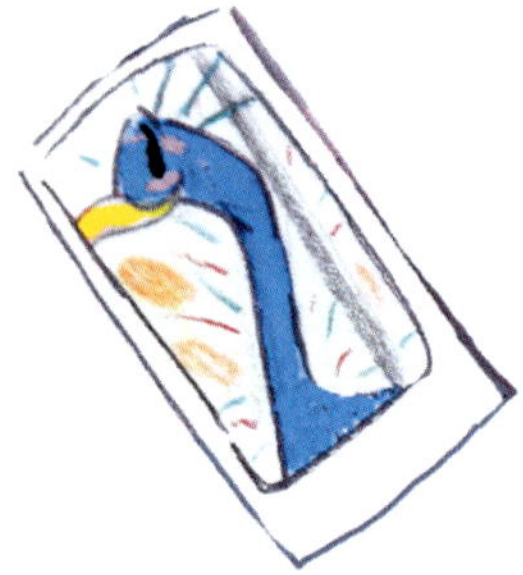

The Prince smiled broadly at this show,
At once took out his phone.
And took a picture of the bird,
Penned in his cage alone.

"Tell me," asked the Prince just then,
"Why is your peacock in a cage?"

"He would have screamed all through your speech
And taken centre stage."

The Prince he understood the point,
He smiled and wandered on.
And Pablo's tail began to droop,
Now that the pair had gone.

The keeper opened-up the cage,
To let the peacock out.
And Pablo flew back to the stage,
To scream and stamp and shout.

When he'd got it off his chest,
A crow came in to land.
A massive regal shiny bird,
A raven tall and grand.

"Feel better?" asked the wise old bird,
"It's something we all learn.
We're not important all the time,
We have to take our turn."

In later days, a letter came,
Which bore the royal crest.
It also came with money,
And an interesting request.

Dear Alice,
I have been asked to thank you, and all the staff at Chester Abbey Park for agreeing to re-home one of the Queen's peacocks, Pedro.
The Queen was interested to learn that you have a peacock of similar disposition and hope that both peacocks find companionship and happiness in Chester Abbey Park.
The Queen has enclosed a cheque to help build a suitable peacock shed for them both and sends her best wishes.
Yours sincerely,
Simon Samuel
Simon Samuel
The Chief Clerk to The Queen

"The ground staff at my residence,
Are driven round the bend.
By a certain show-off peacock,
Would Pablo like a friend?"

"Accept this cheque to build a home,
So Pablo and his friend,
Can show off to each other,
So both learn in the end."

At first these birds did not get on,
They argued and they pecked.
But battles soon exhausted them,
And both birds learnt respect.

Pablo and his friend Pedro,
Are called birds of a feather.
They're quieter than they used to be,
And get on well together.

What do you think?

What does Pablo do to get people to notice him?

Why were people putting up bunting in the park?

How did Pablo behave?
Why do you think he behaved like that?

What could you do if no one is listening to you?
Is it different for home compared to school?

Why did the Queen send a letter to Chester Abbey Park?

Do you think this was a good idea? Why?